21st
Century
Skills Library

ANIMAL INVADERS

STARLING

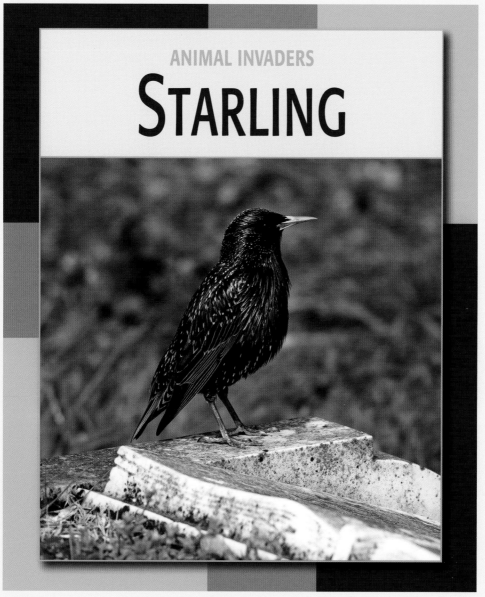

Susan H. Gray

Cherry Lake Publishing
Ann Arbor, Michigan

Published in the United States of America by Cherry Lake Publishing
Ann Arbor, MI
www.cherrylakepublishing.com

Please note: Our map is as up-to-date as possible at the time of publication.

Photo Credits: Cover and page 1, © iStockphoto.com/Whiteway; page 4, © Andrei Volkovets, used under license from Shutterstock, Inc.; page 6, © Joe Gough, used under license from Shutterstock, Inc.; page 9, © Renee Morris/Alamy; page 10, © INTERFOTO Pressebildagentur/Alamy; page 12, © Maslov Dmitry, used under license from Shutterstock, Inc.; page 14, © Joe Goodson, used under license from Shutterstock, Inc.; page 17, © Juniors Bildarchiv/Alamy; page 18, © iStockphoto.com/MikeRega; page 20, © David Tipling/Alamy; page 22, © iStockphoto.com/Chitta; page 25, © Scott Rothstein, used under license from Shutterstock, Inc.; page 26, © Maksym Gorpenyuk, used under license from Shutterstock, Inc.

Map by XNR Productions Inc.

Library of Congress Cataloging-in-Publication Data
Gray, Susan Heinrichs.
Starling / by Susan H. Gray.
    p. cm.—(Animal invaders)
ISBN-13: 978-1-60279-113-8
ISBN-10: 1-60279-113-9
1. Starlings—Juvenile literature. I. Title. II. Series.
QL696.P278G73 2008
598.8'63—dc22   2007035727

*Cherry Lake Publishing would like to acknowledge the work of
The Partnership for 21st Century Skills.
Please visit www.21stcenturyskills.org for more information.*

TABLE OF CONTENTS

CHAPTER ONE

MOVING DAY

A European starling is checking out a new nesting place. It is in the hollow of a dead tree. Insects are plentiful. There is certainly no shortage of food, and plenty of other starlings live nearby. It's the perfect place to live. The songbird gets busy making its nest.

An adult European starling pokes its head out of a tree hole.

Suddenly, a woodpecker lands on the old tree and begins making a fuss. It flaps its wings and calls loudly. It hops back and forth, then jumps right up to the starling. It flaps wildly and lunges at the starling. The woodpecker can't let this happen. The starling has moved into its nest!

The starling holds its ground. It flaps its wings and makes a racket. The starling keeps it up and finally the woodpecker backs off. It flies off to another tree nearby. The woodpecker takes one last look at its old home and then flies away.

21st Century Content

European starlings are often called an invasive species. A species is a particular kind of plant or animal. Starlings, American robins, and eastern bluebirds are different bird species. Something is invasive if it has come into an area and taken over. Human activity usually brings in invasive species.

Invasive species also do some sort of damage to the environment, economy, or human health of a region. For example, European starlings—an invasive species in North America—have caused problems for other wildlife as well as created economic challenges for farmers.

CHAPTER TWO

THE LIFE OF THE EUROPEAN STARLING

The starling's feathers flash purple, blue, green, and bronze colors when the light is just right.

The European starling—*Sturnus vulgaris*—goes by many names. It is also called the common starling, the English starling, or just the starling. It is sometimes called a blackbird, though it is not related to this animal.

The starling is a small bird, about 8.5 inches (21.6 centimeters) long. It weighs only about 2.5 to 3.5 ounces (70 to 100 grams). That's about what a small lemon weighs! It is a black bird with iridescent feathers. These feathers reflect different colors as the bird turns in the sunlight.

The bird has a short, square tail. Its wings are black and pointed. Young birds and those that have just molted have white speckles on their bodies.

The starlings' songs feature a range of remarkable sounds. The sounds that starlings make include clear whistles, squeaks, loud screeches, grating rattles, high-pitched trills, clicks, wheezes, and chirps. Starlings can also imitate the sounds of other birds such as the killdeer, the American robin, the wood thrush, and the American crow. They have even been known to imitate human speech.

European starlings eat all sorts of foods. Worms and insects make up about half of their diet. They probe the ground with their open beaks to get at these foods. They also eat seeds, fruits, berries, grapes, tomatoes, and even table scraps when available.

These birds nest in just about every place imaginable. They make their homes in trees, bushes, attics, barns, and cracks in buildings. They often take over the nests of other birds. They will spot nests created by woodpeckers or bluebirds and run the owners away. Then they set up home in these nests, sometimes adding twigs or grasses to make them more suitable.

This starling rests on a wooly sheep at a farm.

Starlings can be quite creative in choosing a place to nest. One starling was reported to have built a nest in a living sheep's wool!

The females lay their pale blue-green eggs in the spring and summer. They lay four to six eggs at a time, which hatch in about two weeks. In another three weeks, the young are big and strong enough to leave the nest.

Starling eggs rest in a nest of dried grass, sticks, and other plant materials.

Starlings usually raise two broods a year. In the wild, most birds live only a few years. However, there are reports of starlings that lived to be more than 20 years old.

Starlings often gather into huge flocks and set up regular roosting areas. Roosts are places where the birds rest every evening or build nests.

A roost might be made up only of starlings. Or it might also include blackbirds, grackles, and cowbirds. Roosts with hundreds of thousands of birds are not unusual. As the sun sets, the birds fly into the roost, creating a din of loud clicks, rattles, squawks, and whistles.

European starlings live in all sorts of places. They are equally at home in the city and the country. They live near lakes, rivers, ponds, and marshes. They also gather in forests, grasslands, prairies, and farmlands. They can survive in very cold areas, such as parts of northern Canada and Alaska. However, they cannot survive in the heat and don't live where it is extremely hot and humid.

Learning & Innovation Skills

European starlings, like other birds, have songs and calls. A song is usually longer, sometimes musical, and more complicated than a call. Calls, on the other hand, are short and loud. They may be only one or two notes. Calls are often used to warn other birds that danger is near. Why is it better for calls to be short and loud rather than long and musical?

CHAPTER THREE

HOW THE STARLINGS TOOK OVER

Starlings are social birds that often rest on wires in groups.

Years ago, the European starling lived only in Europe, Asia, and North Africa. It was not until the 1890s that the bird came to North America. How did this happen?

It happened with the help of one bird lover in America. In the 1800s, many Europeans looking for new opportunities came to the United States. They often brought plants and animals with them. These weren't just ordinary houseplants and pets. Sometimes, they were rare or unusual plants, wild birds, and other small animals that reminded the Europeans of home.

In those days, no one was too worried that a favorite plant might spread. And no one imagined that a beloved family pet might force native animals from their homes.

In 1890, though, things got a little out of hand. A man in New York had the idea of bringing many different birds to the United States. It has been said that he wanted to bring over every bird that was ever mentioned by his favorite author—the English dramatist and poet William Shakespeare.

A huge flock of starlings looks for a place to roost at sunset.

The man's name was Eugene Schieffelin. He went to England and brought back small birds called skylarks. He released the skylarks, hoping they would thrive in their new home. But the skylarks did not survive.

Then he tried European starlings. In 1890, he released 60 starlings in New York City's Central Park. In 1891, he freed 40 more.

For the next few years, the birds stayed in New York City. They raised their young and those young stayed. But then, the starlings began spreading out. Over the next 80 years, they made their way throughout all of the United States, even to Alaska.

North America is not the only place where humans introduced starlings. In Australia and New Zealand, people brought starlings in to control insect pests. As it turned out, the starlings themselves became the pests! Just as in North America, they settled in and spread quickly.

Over the years, people brought them into a number of other countries. Today, the birds live in North America, New Zealand, Australia, South Africa, Fiji, and Jamaica. In North America, they have done especially well. Almost one-third of the world's starlings live on this continent.

CHAPTER FOUR

THE PROBLEM WITH STARLINGS

A European starling competes with other kinds of birds at a feeder.

Europeans starlings are just one of hundreds of different bird species in North America. They live alongside other birds, eating many of the same foods. They help control populations of some pests such as clover weevils and

Starlings roost on top of a brick building in North America.
They sometimes roost with native bird species.

Japanese beetles. They are sometimes kept as pets. They can even entertain people with their sounds. So why are European starlings considered animal invaders?

Starlings are animal invaders because they can take over just about anywhere they live. They can move in by the thousands. They multiply quickly, having two and even three broods each year.

In places where many different kinds of birds have lived together for years, things change after the starlings move in. Bluebirds and martins go elsewhere to find food. After being forced from their nests, woodpeckers move away. With more room and more food, the starlings continue to expand their range.

European starlings also cause problems for people, crops, and farm animals. Starlings feed on corn, wheat, and other planted grains. They visit fruit trees to eat peaches,

Starlings are not the only invasive bird in the United States. In the northeast, mute swans are invaders. Wealthy homeowners brought in these swans from Europe to enhance the beauty of their large estates. Some of the birds escaped and moved to area lakes and marshes. As soon as the mute swans settled in, the problems began. They chased away the native birds and ate their food. They uprooted water plants that provided safety for fish.

Government officials are trying to control the swan population. Some citizens are angry about those efforts. Not everyone feels the same way about animal invaders. Government bodies, animal-rights groups, and local communities must work together to find solutions to their animal invader problems.

Starlings feed on many kinds of fruit, including apples.

apples, and cherries. A large flock of starlings can damage or destroy gardens, fields, vineyards, and orchards.

The birds also go after livestock feed. When farmers and ranchers put out grain for their cattle, sheep, horses, or chickens, they can expect the starlings to visit. The birds will gorge on the food and foul it with their droppings.

This increases costs for the farms and ranches as well as their customers.

So why aren't starlings a problem in Europe? There the starling's natural enemies are squirrels, hawks, and cats, the same as in the United States and many other countries. But the starlings have been in Europe for many years. Over time, the starlings have reached a balance with their predators and their populations no longer increase year after year.

CHAPTER FIVE

Looking for Answers

*Where they don't belong, animal invaders like the European
starling make survival difficult for native species.*

As soon as people realized that starlings were animal
invaders, they began working on ways to get rid of them.
However, no plan has worked so far. Today, at least 200
million starlings live in North America, and the number
is growing.

Some eradication plans have worked, but only for a short while. People have tried shooting and trapping the birds, but these methods don't show much promise.

Shooting removes only one bird at a time from the population. And firing a gun in cities and towns is dangerous and against the law. Trapping is expensive and requires a lot of time. People have to buy and set the traps, then check on them often. It is likely that they will trap birds other than starlings. Those birds may overheat or starve before someone can check on them.

Most people have decided that it is impossible to get rid of the starlings or even to reduce their numbers. Therefore, many are just trying to drive away the birds. They hope to discourage the birds from settling near their homes, farms, and businesses.

To do this, some people have used "scare" methods. Scarecrows, for instance, have been used for years.

However, because they do not look lifelike and do not move, the starlings get used to them. People have also tried putting plastic owls, hawks, and snakes in their yards and gardens. These may scare the starlings away for a day or two, but the birds soon learn to ignore them.

Moving objects seem to work better. Balloons, kites shaped like hawks, and shiny streamers appear to unsettle the starlings. Ribbons of a thin, shiny film called Mylar posted near starling roosts work well. They flap around in the slightest breeze, touching and flicking the birds, causing them to leave and roost elsewhere.

Certain sounds seem to drive the birds away. Devices that produce loud pops and bangs can scare starlings away for days at a time. However, the birds usually learn that these sounds are harmless, and they return. Furthermore,

Some people have tried using plastic owls to drive away starlings. They have not had much success.

most people do not want such loud devices in their neighborhoods. They cannot endure the sounds for long.

European starlings call to each other in times of danger.

Recordings of starling calls work a little better. Starlings call to warn each other that danger is near. Recordings of such calls can be put on a computer chip. When played loudly from time to time, they can keep the starlings alarmed and at a distance.

Farmers and ranchers have come up with a few simple tricks for keeping the birds away. Some feed their cattle late in the afternoon, when starlings are not very active. Others use bird-proof feeders for their pigs. Still others adjust the water level in troughs, so that it is too low for starlings to reach but not too low for livestock to drink.

Of course, simply keeping starlings away is not a long-term solution. It merely drives them somewhere else. Having introduced starlings outside of their natural range, humans have to work on better solutions. For now, it seems the starlings are here to stay.

Learning & Innovation Skills

In many U.S. states, it is illegal to poison starlings. Poisons tend to stay inside a bird's body. They move into the bird's fatty tissue instead of moving out in the bird's droppings. Other animals that eat the starlings then get a dose of the poison. Poisoning is dangerous for other reasons. What might some of those reasons be?

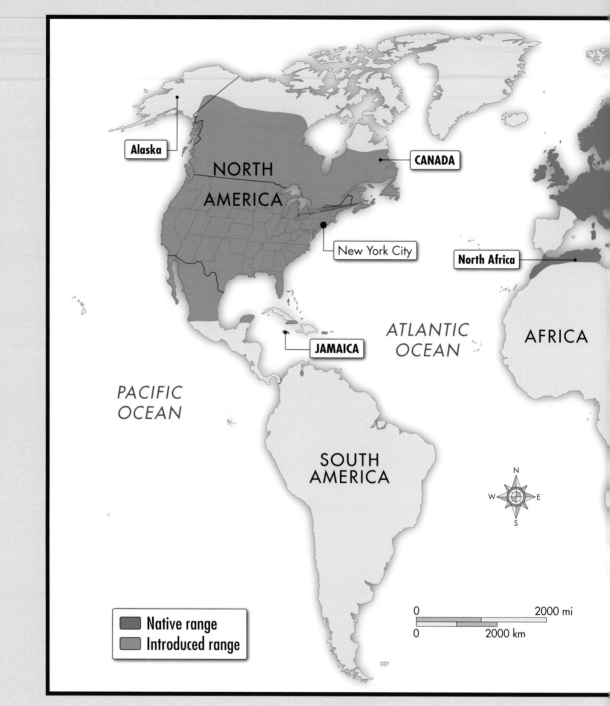

Alaska

NORTH
AMERICA

CANADA

New York City

North Africa

JAMAICA

ATLANTIC
OCEAN

AFRICA

PACIFIC
OCEAN

SOUTH
AMERICA

N
W · E
S

0   2000 mi
0   2000 km

■ Native range
■ Introduced range

This map shows where in the world the European starling

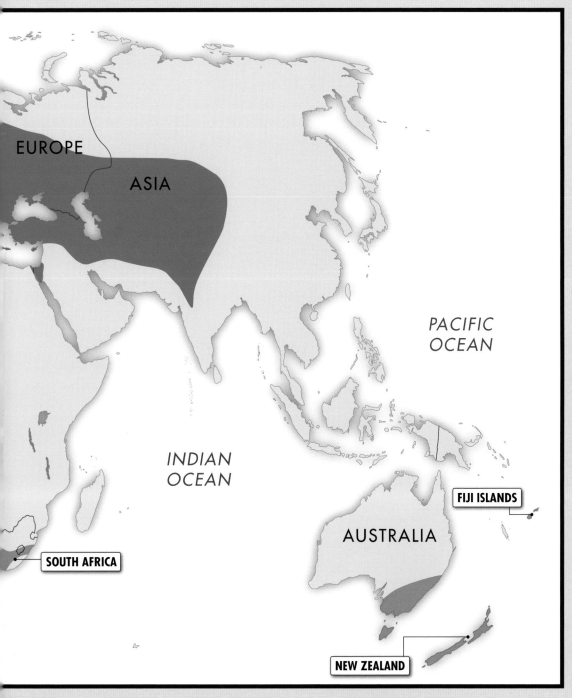

EUROPE

ASIA

PACIFIC
OCEAN

INDIAN
OCEAN

FIJI ISLANDS

AUSTRALIA

SOUTH AFRICA

NEW ZEALAND

lives naturally and where it has invaded.

Glossary

broods (BROODZ) groups of chicks that hatch at the same time

carnivores (KAR-nih-vorz) animals that eat mostly meat

eradication plans (ee-rad-ih-KAY-shun PLANZ) programs of action to get rid of something completely

herbivores (UR-buh-vorz) animals that eat mostly plants

iridescent (ear-eh-DES-ent) showing a display of bright colors

molted (MOLE-ted) shed old feathers to grow new ones

omnivores (OM-nuh-vorz) animals that eat both plants and meat

predators (PRED-uh-turz) animals that hunt and eat other animals

roosts (ROOSTS) places where birds rest or build nests

species (SPEE-sheez) a group of similar plants or animals

troughs (TRAWFS) long, narrow containers that hold water or food for animals

FOR MORE INFORMATION

Books

Beletsky, Les. *Bird Songs: 250 North American Birds in Song*. San Francisco: Chronicle Books, 2006.

Burnie, David. *Bird*. New York: DK Publishing, 2004.

May, Suellen. *Invasive Terrestrial Animals*. New York: Chelsea House, 2007.

Web Sites

All About Birds
www.birds.cornell.edu/AllAboutBirds/BirdGuide/European_Starling.html
For more about starlings on this site run by the Cornell Lab of Ornithology

Global Invasive Species Database
www.issg.org/database/species/ecology.asp?si=74&fr=1&sts=sss
To get more details about the lives, habitats, and impacts of the European starling

National Geographic News
news.nationalgeographic.com/news/2001/01/bioinvasion_2001-01-23.html
For an excellent article about various invasive species, including starlings

INDEX

ABOUT THE AUTHOR

Susan H. Gray has a master's degree in zoology. She has written more than 70 science and reference books for children, and especially loves writing about animals. Gray also likes to garden and play the piano. She lives in Cabot, Arkansas, with her husband, Michael, and many pets.

WATCHUNG LIBRARY
12 STIRLING ROAD
WATCHUNG, NJ 07069